A Man With No Teeth Serves Us Breakfast

poems by Rick Lupert

A Man With No Teeth Serves Us Breakfast

Copyright © 2007 by Rick Lupert
All rights reserved

Ain't Got No Press

Design, and Layout ~ Rick Lupert
Photographs ~ Rick Lupert
Author Photo ~ Addie Lupert

Thanks to Addie, Gregory and Mary, John at the Bar, the concierges at the Holiday Inn Kensington Forum, Jess Gold, The townships of East Ham and West Norwood, Brendan, The Let's Go travel book people, The Queen of England

No part of this book may be used or reproduced in any manner whatsoever without written permission from the author except in the case of brief quotations embodied in critical articles and reviews. But why be so critical? You should meet a nice girl, settle down in the Hamptons. Become a doctor or marry one. Either Way. For more information or to contact the author for any reason try:

(818) 904-1021

or

15522 Stagg Street
Van Nuys, CA 91406

or

Rick@PoetrySuperHighway.com

or

http://PoetrySuperHighway.com/

First CreateSpace Edition ~ June, 2008

Printed by CreateSpace.com
United States of America

ISBN: 978-0-9727555-9-7 $10.00

This book is not dedicated to Jack the Ripper

Introduction

Next to being burned in effigy, having my voice amplified or walking through a door marked PRIVATE, there's nothing I enjoy more than reading new poetry by Rick Lupert. Next to that would have to be reading 'old' poetry by Rick Lupert, immediately followed by causing a scene at a funeral. Whenever I have the chance to travel great distances over bodies of water with ice floating on them, I always bring a collection of Lupert's work. It isn't just to pass the considerable time it takes to even find icebergs so you can fly over them, but to link my legacy with his. You see, I often fly great distances over bodies of water with ice floating on them and I expect one day to be killed by having done so once too often. Scientists and engineers alike all agree (though sometimes you have to get them liquored up beforehand) 600 tons of metal is slightly heavier than air. Eventually some captain is gonna get cocky and try to impress a steward by attempting a manoeuvre he saw in a cartoon and when the smoke clears I want the triage team to find me with Rick Lupert's poetry in my cold, dead hands. Or even my blackened, crispy hands. Or just sort of hugged to my pulverised chest by a couple of stumps. I want some airline spokesperson to present a volume of Rick Lupert's poetry to my family and say "This was found in Mr. Constantine's cold, dead, blackened, crispy, completely severed hands. I'm sure he would want you to have it." Wow, I'm like really depressed all of a sudden. You know what else? The title of this book is *A Man With No Teeth Serves Us Breakfast.* How depressing is that? Come to think of it, when I originally spoke to Rick about writing this introduction, I asked him how many teeth he had and he didn't even know. Then, after I agreed to hold so he could count, he comes back and says "I count twenty eight, does that sound right?" How in God's name am I supposed to know? And yet he expects us to perceive some sort of irony in the fact that a waiter in London (a city in a country where this book is partially set and which is at some great distance from America, across a body of water with Greenland floating on it) has no apparent teeth? Well, we'll let that go for now. You read the book and tell me what you think. That is, if I haven't already been horribly killed as a result of plumiting toward the earth from thousands of feet in the sky. Then you'll have to tell somebody else. And when you find that someone else, rest assured that my family will be reading my charred or water damaged copy of this book and making up their own minds.

Brendan Constantine
Los Angeles
April 30, 2007

Boston ~ July 3-6, 2006

"Imagine a world in which your whole possession is one raspberry and you give it to your friend"

- Boston Holocaust Memorial

LAX

Riding over Boston water
I remember LAX
where a little girl
in terminal four
asked her mother

Are we going where we were?

And they were
And they went

It's all they need, little girls
Reassurance that the future
will bring something familiar

Riding The T

I am disappointed to learn
the spokesperson isn't
Mr. T

Location Identified

From the train we pass by a place where
they manufacture bus stops.

Not the bus stop signs or benches, but the glass booths
that house the benches

and keep the free schedules
dry.

I guess
they have to manufacture those somewhere.

Tired

I haven't slept or showered
in three time zones

I smell like the oldest clock
in America

I will sleep through
the revolution

She Knows Better

On the fourth of July
I wore red, white and blue

American Flag Underwear.
So I didn't think it would be a problem

during the fireworks
near the Charles River

if I pulled down my pants
and shouted God Bless America!

My wife assured me
it would be.

Breakfunch

We discover meal between breakfast and brunch.
Breakfunch, we call it. Eating eggs and egg whites
and pancakes and real maple syrup bottled straight
from tree in kitchen. Addie says I don't know what
happens when 'blueberries become inside pancakes'
and then more, but this phrasing has me thinking
existentially about blueberries appearing, like birth,
inside pancakes. The bookstore cafe. Where life begins.
We wait for phone calls and more of Boston

London ~ July 7-16, 2006

"The least one can ask of a sculpture is that it does not move"

- Salvador Dali

"The exquisite corpse will drink the young wine."

- Collectively produced sentence
Tate Modern - 1925

Les Escargots: Un Instrument Erotique

(The snakes: an erotic instrument)

The Dali Lithographic where
the woman has snails
instead of breasts.

I tell Addie
If she ever develops this condition
She should see a doctor

immediately.

Going in the Queen's Gallery

I

Once again I am peeing
in Her Royal Majesty's men's bathroom

II

Wouldn't it be nice if I could
write something about Buckingham Palace
without referring to peeing?

III

That last poem says it all
doesn't it?

IV

Yes

The Finchley Experience

I return to Finchley
It took one too many trains
Walk up the main street
past every Indian Restaurant
and one with giant sign:
VEGETARIAN RESTAURANT

Hungry like a jacket potato
Meet old friend and her parents
Drive to other Finchley house
without parents
Dine in new house with
eight people and one cat

Cat is only one who lives in house
Two others are only half people
Everyone is from different country
Soon will travel to even other countries
Songs are sung
Dessert is eaten

Second dessert, only good English chocolate
Third dessert, a single strawberry
Half person taunts resident cat
Sing more songs. Promise of future night.
Two trains back to town
The right number of trains

Entitled to a Beer: Language Barrier I

Tonight we are brave enough to enter the hotel bar
We were told last night you could only drink after eleven
if you were a resident. It took us all day to realize
they meant a hotel resident, and not a resident of London

Wrong Body

After the fourth of July in Boston
We find ourselves in Westminster Abby
and the tomb of King George The Third

I guess that whole America thing
didn't work out too well for him

John at the Bar

Not the one from the Billy Joel song
but the one from Liverpool
recommends the bitter

So I order a pint
We talk of Texas and 9/11
He sells large empty liquid containers
in German, French and English

He says he'll see us at breakfast
I don't have the heart to tell him
I haven't seen breakfast since Clinton left office

We say our goodbyes then float up the elevator like
a half pint liquid container
overflowed with a pint

Observation

All the women in London
look like the queen

All the men
look British

I Am Become Super Hero

Because of one of my accidents
We buy instant stain remover in Boston

I spend the rest of London
with the stick in my pocket

like a super hero whose
arch villains are stains

Conversation In Bed

I can't sleep.

Why not count sheep?

No.

How about leopards?

No.

Giraffes?

Sigh, that will take a while.

While on a London Walk

We spend an evening in Hampstead
discussing religion with a couple from Pittsburgh
dining on food from Morocco. There is always
common ground with food.

Arch Villain Attacks

I cough out chocolate onto my white shirt
at eight o-clock in the morning
Captain Instant Stain Remover to the Rescue!
Oh yes, Rub Captain, Rub.

Protected by Duck

Leaving London to see castles and cliffs
Our tour guide is a plastic umbrella with a duck head
We're in especially good shape, but
only if it rains

A True Story

One day
a man with
no teeth
serves us
breakfast

English Degrees

I am hot and cold
I am as undecided as the weather on this island

My sleeves are wet
My shirt is white

I am on a bus with forty other people
of varying temperatures

They say we can control the wind
but we find the buttons are for show

And so, we are the temperature that we are
Dressed in layers, mostly skin

We are in for a lovely day and
a certain number of degrees and

things that will go in our mouths
as the wind blows through our hair

as uncontrollable as
a driver on a London Bus

The Holding Rock

At the beach
the beach made of rocks
The beach made of rocks under the cliffs
The white cliffs of Dover
The Dover with a castle on top of the cliffs
The castle built on Roman ruins
The ruins built on prehistoric settlement
The settlement whose settlers
would walk on the beach
The beach with the stones
Dover Beach
Addie picked up a handful of stones
All fell away but one
She kept this one
Called it her holding rock
Said it was good to hold
Said it was comfortable to hold
Until the guilt came
The guilt of taking the rock
The guilt of *what if everyone took a rock*
The twisting of the stone in her hand
The comfortable stone
The holding stone
She'll put it on a grave someday
She rubs it in her hand and hums
The cliffs of Dover
The beach
The stones

Three things My Wife Said

I

I'm like juice-pea happy!

II

Is that poppycock?
(referring to the flower which
may or may not have been
a hollyhock)

III

Do I have mud and gross goo on my bum?

How the Red Army Spent Our Whole Morning

If I ran the changing of the guard
It would only take five minutes
and everyone would be in the front row

Tea at the Thistle

Quite lovely
except for the moth
and the dead fly

Luxury in Any Country

is a plate of assorted cheese.
Even in this country, England
where the Kir is not good
but, by God, at least there's Kir.

We have just seen Mary Poppins.
So naturally we're wondering if
our travel cards cover umbrella.

There are never enough biscuits with
assorted cheese plates and certainly
don't I mean bread? But no. This is London
and God is in the bakery cellars of Paris
monitoring the progress of future baguettes.

So we crunch with celery, nature's biscuit
with cheese so stinky it makes us smile
even amidst a waiter so rude, his tip floats
out of his hands like an umbrella.

We will fly all night
or at least until the Underground closes
when we'll be back in the room with the curtains
that make the daylight go away.

Language Barrier II

The word "fanny," in England, is slang for Vagina.
This isn't so much a poem as a public service
to the those of you who might travel here and
need a polite way to refer to your ass.

Two Observations

Addie's Observation

The signs which read "To Let" everywhere mean
there is a space for rent in the building.
Addie sees it as the word "toilet, with a missing "I".
She asks if I am proud of this observation
Oh yes, Addie, I am.

Rick's Observation

Wouldn't it be funny if the letter "I"
was removed from the Toilet signs
and people came along with their furniture
and first months rent?

At Windsor Castle: The Right Body

We tread over the tomb of King George The Third
Resist all urges to leave tea-bags
and thumb our noses and say things like
ha ha, we're American and you're dead.

Our tour guide tells us this George was soft in the head
like a baby only with no chance for future development.
Tonight there will be a masquerade ball.

George, here in the castle, your great great great grand
something or other is turning eighteen. They say
everyone in England pays seventy pence a year
to support the monarchy. George, your splendid houses
and horses and horse houses.

We're your best friend too now.
Don't mind my feet. This plaque probably just covers
a large chamber befitting a you, George,
and not actually the remains of your nose or eyebrows.

I should show you more respect,
walk around, perhaps to the left.
You didn't know any better, your soft head.
I'll leave a few pence with the Bishop.

Lifelong Dream

for Homer Simpson and Roy Orbison

It has always been my lifelong dream
to open a pub in my city
build a Stonehenge in my backyard
live on a clipper ship
have elephants and castles
on every corner

My lifelong dream has always been
to travel in a dumb waiter
install a moat
have a train stop underneath my house
understand the difference between beer and beer

If I were to tell you my lifelong dream
you'd hear how I wanted to
walk across bridges every day
build a miniature replica of every building and object
be a gentleman of leisure
have a past worth mentioning

My lifelong dream is to have a lifelong dream
live in a house made of wood and stone and marble and wood
interact with chimpanzees

In lifelong dreams I walk with you
In lifelong dreams I talk with you

Airplane Noise and it's Effect on the Monarchy

I can't imagine the Queen had much to say
about the path of landing airplanes over Windsor Castle

The triple paned glass on her private rooms there
She had everything to do with that.

Daily

They change
the guard here
like underwear.

The Best Course of Action

We've spent two days
following women with umbrellas
outside of London

One umbrella
looked like a duck
and was called Cedrick

The second
looked like nothing and was called
The Stick of Punishment

We tipped well
and avoided
all contact

Language Barrier III *

They tell us the hotel pub
is only for residents after eleven PM
We find out days later
they meant Hotel not Neighborhood.
We mourn the beers we never had

* *The author would like you to pretend that you did not read the similar poem on page 20 before you begin reading this poem. Thank you.*

Haiku

With names like Thistle
Chiswick and Cockfosters, it's
got to be good jam.

Watching Sports on the Tele

Oh yeah London?
We feed cricket
to our lizard.

Erotic Deception

This is not a beer belly
It's two weeks in London
Travel the world with me
baby

We Don't Recommend It

In London
the train network is so extensive
you could take it up other people's asses
if you wanted

Accommodating Our Diet

Restaurants here
have a standard of putting
a distinguishable "V"
by menu items which are vegetarian.
I feel so welcome here,

until I remember the show "V"
about the lizard aliens
disguised as humans
who came to take over the world
and eat us.

I spend the next five days
in my hotel room
ordering room service
and disguised as
not lizard food.

Addie Speaks at Breakfast

You put something close to my lips
I'm either going to eat it
or kiss it.

The Final Bitter

and the last train has rolled away
I saw the lights disappear into the tunnel
up the escalator
through the turnstile
down the road
into the hotel
the pub
and this final bitter
London Pride
Smooth and warm down my throat
like London
Unseasonably warm
where all weather is typical
Naturally carbonated
like an ancient hot spring
covered in a ruined Roman Bath
covered by a Georgian Facade
covered by a museum.
It is impossible to see everything anywhere.
So we did what we could
Saw things the locals hadn't heard of
(Isn't that always the case,
we become so familiar with our home towns,
we have no idea what's interesting about them?)
So it's a few pounds in our pockets
a four AM car to the plane
This final bitter
golden
Cheerio
Bring that chair here
Carry me home

About The Author

The Author chopping off his own head at the Klink Museum in London

Rick Lupert has been involved in the Los Angeles poetry community since 1990. He served for two years as a co-director of the Valley Contemporary Poets, a twenty-five year old non-profit organization which produces a readings and publications out of the San Fernando Valley. His poetry has appeared in numerous magazines and literary journals, including *The Los Angeles Times, Chiron Review, Stirring, PoeticDiversity.org, Zuzu's Petals, Caffeine Magazine, Blue Satellite* and others. He is the author of 10 other books: *Paris: It's The Cheese, I Am My Own Orange County, Mowing Fargo, I'm a Jew. Are You?, Stolen Mummies, I'd Like to Bake Your Goods,* (Ain't Got No Press), *Lizard King of the Laundromat, Brendan Constantine is My Kind of Town* (Inevitable Press), *Feeding Holy Cats* and *Up Liberty's Skirt* (Cassowary Press). He has hosted the long running Cobalt Café reading series in Canoga Park since 1994 and is regularly featured at venues throughout Southern California.

Rick created and maintains the Poetry Super Highway, a major internet resource for poets. (http://PoetrySuperHighway.com/)

Currently Rick works as the music teacher and graphic and web designer for Temple Ahavat Shalom in Northridge, CA and for anyone who would like to help pay his mortgage.

Rick's Other Books

I'd Like to Bake Your Goods
Ain't Got No Press
January, 2006

STOLEN MUMMIES
Ain't Got No Press
February, 2003

BRENDAN CONSTANTINE IS
MY KIND OF TOWN
Inevitable Press
September, 2001

up liberty's skirt
Cassowary Press
March, 2001

FEEDING HOLY CATS
Cassowary Press
May, 2000

I'm a Jew, Are You?
Cassowary Press
May, 2000

MOWING FARGO
Sacred Beverage Press
December, 1998

Lizard King of the Laundromat
The Inevitable Press
February, 1998

I Am My Own Orange County
Ain't Got No Press
May, 1997

Paris: It's The Cheese
Ain't Got No Press
May, 1996

For more information: http://PoetrySuperHighway.com/